# Victory Is Mine Evidence Tartt

# Victory Is Mine Evidence Tartt

> I, THE LORD GOD-GREAT AND MIGHTY, will be with Raiden in Trouble; THE LORD GOD-GREAT AND MIGHTY will Deliver Raiden, and Honour Raiden.
>
> Psalm 91:15b (emphasis added)

Evidence Tartt

Chapter 13 Publishing LLC

Chapter 13 Publishing LLC

**VICTORY IS MINE**

Copyright © 2020 by EVIDENCE TARTT.
This book is also available as an e-book.
Visit **www.chapter13publishing.com.**

All rights reserved. Printed in the United States of America. No part of this book may be used or reproduced in any manner whatsoever, stored in a retrieval system, or transmitted in any form or by an means—electronic, mechanical, photocopy, recording, or any other—except for brief quotations in printed reviews, without the prior permission of the publisher.

Requests for information should be addressed to:
**Chapter 13 Publishing LLC**
For information contact:
**Chapter13pub@gmail.com**

Scripture taken from the New King James Version®. Copyright © 1982 by Thomas Nelson. Used by permission. All rights reserved.
Chapter titles taken from Life Changing Music Album © ? on recording, artwork, photos; 2006 by EMI Gospel Records (employer for hire) and Smokie Norful. All rights reserved.

Book and Cover design by Ebony "Evidence" Tartt
ISBN: 978-1-7354736-1-1
EISBN: 978-1-7354736-0-4

First Edition: June 2020

# CONTENTS

| | | |
|---|---|---|
| ACKNOWLEDGEMENT | | vii |
| INTRODUCTION | | ix |
| 1 | Celebrate | 1 |
| 2 | Um Good | 3 |
| 3 | Great and Mighty | 11 |
| 4 | Run Til I Finish | 15 |
| 5 | In Time | 19 |
| 6 | More Than Anything | 23 |
| 7 | Where Would I Be | 31 |
| 8 | Put Your Hands Together | 33 |
| 9 | Right Now | 35 |

**CONTENTS**

**10** | Run To You   **41**

**11** | Celebrate—Reprise   **45**

MEET EVIDENCE   **55**

> To My Benevolent Husband:
> Babe I Genuinely LOVE You.

I honor GOD in creating You. In You, GOD created a man that pushes me to better. With You, I grow into the Best version GOD intends me to be. GOD made Your genes so strong that not only did Raiden look like You, but was just as tenacious as You. The wisdom and Love GOD birthed through You are so warm and I now know how tangible it is so that I can live beyond admiration of You, but purposely live out my days habitually seeing the best in each person and being as loving, warm, and wise as You—the ways JESUS expects of us.

# INTRODUCTION

**"GOD said that he is changing you and your son's bloodline."** These words were spoken by my pastor, Bishop Joseph Futch, Jr., as we prepared to leave Wednesday evening bible study. Those words of GOD lingered in my heart for days even until now. At the time. Raiden was still yet in my womb being formed by GOD.

You never know what GOD has in store for your life—even when HE releases prophecies.

*"For we know in part and we prophesy in part"*
**1 Corinthians 13:9 KJV**

But one thing I do know: GOD has the final say and HIS Word is true and pure—and let me not forget to mention that HIS thoughtful words towards HIS children are *"of peace, and not of evil,"* but GOD'S Words *"give an expected end"* **(Jeremiah 29:11 KJV)**.

Where I am today is because of GOD'S Beautiful Grace and Mercy. GOD'S Works are never ugly. If there is something that one may deem ugly, it was not by the hand of GOD!

- Hate is ugly. GOD is the GOD of Love! **(1 John 4:19)**

## INTRODUCTION

- Confusion is ugly and GOD *"is not the author of confusion,"* so therefore HE will not illustrate it. (**1 Corinthians 14:33**)

I am proud to say that GOD IS AWESOME; and though HE never has to, HE Continuously PROVES HIMSELF AS A WAY MAKER!

Five years ago, GOD allowed me to make it to the last chapter in my "Before Christ" book. Though I knew I needed another book, I did not know that I was in the last chapter of the book I had owned, for nearly 24 years. This new, unexpected, book that I would soon have ownership of was not something that my heart longed for at the time. However, my soul was in desperation, waiting twenty-three plus long years for me to take ownership that waited for me free of charge. The book I had lived out so long—all my life to be exact—had a great cost that my soul did not want to have to pay. My flesh, selfishly, racked up a high bill. I was never supposed to keep the book as long as I did. It had gotten so bad that the interest due increased every second. The credit owed on this book included innumerable late fees. My flesh would never had been able to pay the cost on earth. Instead my soul would have paid the debt in the lake of fire, if I died still owning the book. My soul knew that I could never pay this exponential growing debt. But my flesh wanted more reckless adventure, while my soul yearned for the Reckless Love of GOD. I knew I could change books, I knew it since I was a child. I also knew that this book would wipe out all the debt my flesh incurred.

## INTRODUCTION

However, this book was on the bottom of my list of books to pick up from the library. Or so I thought! Though my heart lacked zeal to retrieve the book, I always knew one thing for sure, that once I picked out this book, it would never be returned to the library—borrowing the book was not an option. This new book would no longer reside solely in the library. I would have full ownership of this book!

Little did I know that this book was not at the library that I had been attending all my life. In the words of Eld. Frye, from my local church, "it was time for me to go to another library."

GOD Blessed me to join in Holy Matrimony to the man that saw, recognized, and loved more than I did—for over five years—that my name would not just be registered to his but to this new library that I had been avoiding for far too long.

Two days after we wed, I decided to change libraries. During the altar call, Sunday, February 15, 2015, I made my request known to the Librarian (GOD), received a library card (New Identification), and chose The Book (JESUS).

For too many years, I had my understanding of salvation, but I did not live the life of salvation. On that glorious day, I was a ***"new creature"*** and ***"the old things…passed away"*** and I was made ***"new"*** (**2 Corinthians 5:17 KJV**).

I know timing is more perfect than we, even as GOD'S children could ever fathom. I believe that if I did not take on the Identity as GOD'S child at the time I did, the next years that followed could have ended with me never walking into that New Library.

Praise be to GOD OUR FATHER because HE knows the beginning, middle, and end!

## INTRODUCTION

*When I was YOUR foe, still YOUR LOVE Fought For Me*
*YOU have been so, so good to me*
*When I felt no worth, YOU PAID IT ALL For Me*
*YOU have been so, so kind to me*
*And Oh, The Overwhelming; Never-Ending, Reckless LOVE OF GOD*
*Oh, It Chases me down, Fights 'til I'm Found, Leaves the ninety-nine*
*And I couldn't earn it, and I don't deserve it, still, YOU GIVE YOURSELF AWAY*
*And Oh, The Overwhelming; Never-Ending, Reckless LOVE OF GOD* [1]

# 1

## Celebrate

**On March 15, 2018, at about 7:45 A.M.**, my husband and I were awakened by two things: the bright, beautiful sun rising, and the monitor beeping, indicating that Raiden's heart was decreasing rapidly. The question was: Were we going to Rejoice or be full of Remorse? I cannot recall ever experiencing such a beautiful sunrise. It was Glorious and Powerful. GOD'S Beauty entered Raiden's hospital room and HIS Shine radiated the room. GOD was welcoming us to our new day so we could rejoice and be glad in it, but we quickly had to decide whether we would rejoice despite the minutes that followed.

"I'm sorry his heart has stopped."

These are not the words that I expected to hear about our beautiful, energetic son, Raiden Xzavier Tartt. Our very rambunctious two-year-old son. The same child that said GOD'S Name and Loved to read scriptures from our prayer wall and the bible. Raiden? Who gives these hugs that made you feel like He was comforting and protecting us, when it was us that gave the hug to do the exact thing for him. Not our son.

It was not that I did not believe the doctor's report. But I did not foresee that the next moments would confirm that at that moment in time, his heart would not start and recover. Doing as a mother would do, seeking for a resurrection, I prayed to JESUS. Softly into Raiden's ear, I spoke life over our son.

As I held Raiden, we both, now, were lifeless—he in the natural, myself in the spirit. Sitting in a sofa chair, in this children's ICU room assigned to Raiden, I held him. The chaplain, who had befriended our family, walked in and sat on the hospital bed near my husband. My husband opened his mouth, moved his lips, and began to speak and proclaim the Goodness of GOD. He prayed and thanked GOD for Blessing he and I, family, and friends for such a Marvelous Favorable time to be Graced with our Beautiful Raiden. Me, I was operating in formality, not feeling like Thanking GOD but knowing how to respond in prayer. In the motions. My son had more life to him than I did. This is not a false statement, because although there was no movement in his flesh. His soul was most certainly quickened.

I give GOD the glory that HE did not take me in the state that I was in…for about a week, I operated in the motions and it was pitiful. Towards the cares of the world, I was lively. Towards caring for GOD and doing HIS will, at times I was dull and lifeless. However, I Praise GOD that I serve a GOD not made by man's hands. Not a god that I get to select what his thoughts are. Nope. That is not the GOD I serve.

*"For My Thoughts are not your thoughts, neither are your ways My Ways, saith THE LORD.*
*For as the heavens are higher than the earth, so are MY Ways higher than your ways, and MY Thoughts than your thoughts."*
**Isaiah 55:8-9 KJV**

# 2

## Um Good

**Raiden and I were blessed.** We had much reason to *Celebrate*. There were no mishaps or scares while I carried Raiden for 39 weeks. Every doctor's appointment went great. No concerns. Raiden was growing and so was my tummy: "It was getting bigger, and bigger, and bigger." [1]

When my husband and I discovered I was expecting, I was five months—to the very day—as wife to my husband and days short of five months as a dedicated child of GOD. As months went on, I picked up a second job as a school bus driver. It was great; at work, during downtime, GOD would have me read HIS Glorious Word. At home, I would be found doing many things, again, I would most often be found reading GOD'S Loving Words of Affirmation.

If I am not mistaken, one-day GOD had me read 1 Samuel chapter 1. As I continued to read, I became at awe and admired the woman, Hannah.

Hannah was a woman who seemed to fear GOD and knew that only HE could answer her prayers. She was married to a loving husband, Elkanah. He loved her even despite her not being able to bear children. However, Hannah wanted to bear a child for her husband, and he would remind her, children or no children he loved her regardless. During one of their yearly visits to Shiloh *"to worship and to sacrifice unto THE LORD"* (**1 Samuel 1:3 KJV**), Hannah's spirit was heavy due to being provoked by her Husband's other wife. The other wife belittled Hannah because she bore no children for Elkanah. This made Hannah weep, keeping her from an appetite. She found a place to be alone and prayed to GOD for a son. If it were GOD'S will to bless her womb with a son, Hannah vowed that she would give the child back to GOD to be a Spiritual Servant of HIS. Her words were not spoken aloud, but she mouthed them in silence.

Eli the priest saw her and perceived that she was drunk; Eli inquired about her state of mind and she let him know that she had not been drunk of any drink but was praying to GOD. He told her to *"Go in peace: and the GOD of Israel grant thee thy petition that thou hast asked of HIM"* (**1 Samuel 1:17 KJV**). The result: GOD Blessed Hannah's womb with a son. Hannah raised her son, Samuel, up until she weaned him from being breastfed and then gave Samuel to GOD as she promised.

After reading this passage, I decided that I would do the same: Raiden would be given back to GOD and whatever way GOD wanted to use Raiden I was to accept GOD'S Will. I believe, shortly after Raiden was born, I revisited the passage once again and read it to Raiden. Informing him and reminding myself that Raiden's Life has been Dedicated to GOD. I did not know that in 2017, GOD would remind me this quite often, at least five or more times, as I frequently surrendered my time to HIM as I participated in a Forty Day Surrender Fast written and led by Dr. Celeste Owens.[2]

I cannot say the percentage, but I pray that it was close to 90% that every decision made about Raiden was consulted with GOD and many times there was no movement in decision making until GOD said what to do.

During a Wednesday night bible study, at my local church, the 2nd Assistant Pastor testified that at his job, he met a woman who was bold for CHRIST. He gave examples. I was determined that I would be bold for CHRIST also. I began to pray for boldness. GOD told me to add 'prepare me' to my prayers also. As I continued to pray for boldness and to be prepared, I began to perceive through the Holy Ghost that this preparation was concerning Raiden.

In July 2016, I was forewarned again. This time I was disobedient to the Spirit. {I have since asked for forgiveness.} While shopping for some clothes for Raiden at a store with some amazing deals, I decided to shop for the future. I gathered some clothes that were size 24-months and 2T. GOD placed in my spirit that Raiden would never wear those clothes. But I bought the clothes, anyway, ignoring what was said.

The following month, there were some more things of GOD'S Will I tried to prevent. I am a frequent reader of DAUGHTERS OF THE KING Daily Devotionals.[3] Normally, I read the devotional when GOD tells me to do so. On a certain day in August of 2016, a day I perceived would be normal, was not the "normal" I was expecting. GOD placed in my heart to read the daily devotional, in this devotional it discussed GOD Blessing HIS Children with double. The scriptures to read were found in Job.

I knew GOD was getting me ready and I was like 'Aw, Naw GOD you can't make me read that.' I refused to read it because I knew that Raiden's time was nearing—me now thinking that death was about to take our son.

Another warning came. From May or June until August, I played one of my Smokie Norful CDs over and over. I knew that I was being ministered to, but I did not know that GOD was using this CD, which is titled, "Life Changing," as one of the elements to prepare me. So here I am jamming—I had barely listened to local radio, I was tired of hearing their same songs—but my spirit could not seem to get enough of playing this particular CD, hearing the same songs for minutes or hours a time. GOD knew what I needed. I was able to sing along with every song. Singing the words to every song but hearing the meaning of a few.

Another day in August, listening to the same CD, the next song to play was *UM GOOD*,[4] which has similarities to the story of JOB. Smokie Norful sang to GOD: if YOU take this *and* that away—one of the things being his family—YOU are still good. My spiritual ear (my heart) knew that his words were true; however, my natural ear was like...Uh, Skip! Every time the song came on, it was skipped. Was not playing it. I knew with this uneasiness in my gut—this cannot be denied, but I am going to try to avoid feeling—meant that we were shortly approaching what was to come—Raiden's death.

The second week in August, I woke up Monday morning sick. Raiden was currently being partially fed by my milk supply and canned formula. Not wanting to get Raiden sick, on that day, he solely drank formula bottles. That night, Raiden spiked a fever of over a 100. We call the on-call nurse trying to judge what to do. They said if the fever consisted to bring him to the doctor. I took him to the doctor's office the next day. There they told me that Raiden probably had hand, foot, and mouth virus and we were sent home.

The next week, at night, Raiden spikes another fever over 100 degrees. We called the on-call nurse. The following day we took Raiden, again, to his primary care doctor. Within that week, Raiden loses his appetite, energy, and smile. He becomes lethargic and his breathing becomes abnormal with a wheezing sound.

On either the first or second Sunday of August 2016, Raiden and I attended church. At the end of service, I waited to speak with my pastor to request prayer for Raiden. The wait was extremely long because many people wanted to talk to him. It may have gotten to about forty minutes and I decided to head home. I went to the car and got Raiden strapped in his car seat. The Holy Spirit and the beautiful gift from GOD, mother's intuition, would not allow me to leave the parking lot. I took Raiden back into the church for my pastor to pray for him, I just knew that something was not right in Raiden's body. My pastor prayed for Raiden and told me that he did not want me to worry and stress myself, assuring me that Raiden was fine, and that GOD had him.

Monday August 22nd, Raiden spikes a fever again. I schedule an appointment at the doctor's office for 2 p.m. I was told that if there were any major concerns before the appointment time, I could bring him earlier than the scheduled time to be seen. The next morning, Tuesday, August 23, 2016, I was getting ready to leave the house with Raiden. Before his appointment, I was scheduled around 10 or 11 that morning to choose my route for the upcoming school year, I was still working as a bus driver.

While we were still at home, Raiden was strapped in his car seat and he began to make a choking noise. I knew that bidding for a route would have to be forgotten because I needed to get Raiden to the doctors right away. By the grace of GOD, we made it to the doctors. It was GOD that kept my nerves during the drive there. We made it to the doctor's office, safely. Not too long after arriving, Raiden's name was called to be seen. Raiden is in his stroller and I stroll Raiden into room and the intake nurse sees Raiden and suddenly leaves and brings back, who I am guessing was, a seasoned Nurse. The "Seasoned" nurse looked at Raiden and immediately calls for help. If I am not mistaken, they gave Raiden two breathing treatments and were deciding if it would be wise to send him to the University of Michigan Mott's Children's hospital or to St. Joseph Mercy Hospital. They chose St. Joseph Mercy Hospital which was 10 miles away, three miles less than Mott's. I think they did not think Raiden had much longer to live. BUT GOD!

The ambulance was called. As I waited for EMT to arrive, I was beginning to panic—inwardly, I did not know how to react. My strength to pray seemed to vanish, so I called my spiritual mother, Ms. Angela. She prayed, oh she prayed and I was beginning to receive spiritual consciousness. After getting off the phone with Ms. Angela, I called my other spiritual mother, Missionary Love. She prayed and spoke wisdom into me. From the time I left the doctor's office and during the ride in the ambulance, she remained on the phone with me and told me to get all the crying out. I was frantic. She said, "Get it out now because when you walk in the hospital, the crying is going to have to stop because you need to be calm enough to hear everything the doctor speaks to you. If you have to go to the bathroom and cry, go, but when you come back you have to be calm to hear."

# 3

## Great and Mighty

**I walked into St. Joseph, spiritually, mentally, and physically at peace.** I do not know the order in which I called my family, but the first two calls were essential to my ability to function and hear. I give GOD the Glory for them. Eventually, the rest of the family: my mom, my dad, my husband's parents, one of my husband's sisters, and my husband came to the hospital. The doctor, the nurses, and the chaplain were wonderful. It was a lot to behold, a child days from being six months old, and his parents not knowing the outcome of the next minutes. I was told by the doctor, very gently, but with stern expertise—I am sure, he did not want me to be blindfolded about the seriousness of what was going on—that it was a possibility that Raiden had leukemia. When the word leukemia was spoken my knees buckled a little. But there was no fear. This most certainly was *Um Good* because such a report could only be yielded to CHRIST, allowing the power of THE HOLY GHOST to Take Over.

My pastor told me, days after Raiden's passing, as I spent time with him, his wife, and family, that JESUS went on the cross, but it was CHRIST who was crucified!

JESUS was the man, human, in fleshly body, but CHRIST is the spiritual body. JESUS, on the cross, spoke to GOD and asked, *"Why have you forsaken me"* **(Matthew 27:46 NKJV).**

He was in turmoil and flesh could no longer take the mental and physical agony, but CHRIST could! So, CHRIST took over and finished the assignment on the Cross. Now that I look back that is what happened to me. Flesh could not do it, but due to the Gift that GOD and CHRIST granted me, which is the HOLY GHOST, I was comforted because HE who took over for me. Up until the last week of Raiden's life, THE HOLY GHOST never left my side, destroying all fear and doubt and I Give GOD the GLORY for that!

At St. Joseph Mercy hospital Raiden's white blood count was at 440, 000. After Raiden was stabilized, the St. Joseph Mercy Hospital head emergency doctor felt secure enough to have Raiden transported to the University of Michigan Mott's Children's hospital.

When we got there, Raiden was rushed to the ER surgery room. It is all a blur, but I feel like there were so many white coats, so many stethoscopes, and innumerable conversations. My husband and I stayed in the room while all this occurred, doctors spoke many things that I cannot recall. If I am not mistaken, they were drawing Raiden's blood to have an updated blood count. Before leaving the emergency room, Raiden had a breathing tube, a tube to collect bile, and all sorts of monitors connected to him.

By night-time, Raiden was sedated in a room in the Pediatric ICU. He had been transported hours earlier. Another update was given to our family that Raiden had 660, 000 white blood cells in his body when entering the hospital. BUT GOD! With that many white blood cells, in the minds of the doctors, Raiden should have been dead, or suffering from a stroke, or severe seizure. BUT GOD! We were told the normal range of white blood cells is around 10, 000. BUT GOD!

This all occurred on Tuesday, August 23, 2016. Raiden was five days shy of being 6 months. PRAYER was necessary! Gospel music filling the walls of that room was necessary! Reading the word and devotionals was necessary!

While we were at the hospital, my pastor informed me later that evening at Tuesday night bible study, he called our entire church to prayer and consecration for Raiden for the following three days.

The days that followed, I cannot remember the conversations spoken aloud. But I do know that the majority of us held our own conversation with GOD whether through praise, begging and pleading, questioning, and or making requests known. But I was not taking death for an answer.

While typing this last sentence, I am reminded that this, however, is what the Holy Spirit forewarned me of...but no, I was not living in that Realm concerning the thoughts of our son.

Days went by, but not too many...THANKS BE TO GOD!

# 4

## Run Til I Finish

**The doctors diagnosed Raiden with leukemia.** My reaction that moment and from that moment forward may have baffled others. Because cancer, for the first time, didn't frighten me. I had known many people diagnosed with cancer up to that very day, at least two hands full if not more. GOD prepared me for that day many months prior.

> On one of my field trips, I was blessed to meet a woman who would take children on nature trips. After the field trip, the woman and I began to converse, as I helped her unload her equipment from the bus. In our conversation, she confided in me and told me that her husband had just been diagnosed with cancer. I am just realizing now, as I type, that she was at work while her husband was just diagnosed with cancer.
> This is called operating in faith. She did not let the wiles of the devil stop her everyday life. Why? Because out of her mouth she told me that she believed GOD. Her husband was not the first in her household to be diagnosed with cancer, she too years prior had been diagnosed with cancer and through faith and GOD providing her healing, she was cancer-free! LOOK AT

GOD! I told her that I would most certainly keep them up in prayer. If she did not feel defeated, why should I have forced her to? For we are Victorious through Christ Jesus!

Maybe a month or so later, my neighbor tells me that her husband had just been diagnosed with cancer. GOD used me to pray and continuously encourage her to speak JESUS! This unexpected information did not weigh me down, it just pumped me up to be more excited about the *Great and Mighty* moves of GOD!

As I type, both these men are cancer-free! To GOD Be The Glory!

GOD orchestrated for me to be connected with these women and to be a supporting encourager to them. I was Blessed with the opportunity to speak life and to Trust with them that GOD would do a mighty work for their Husbands.

*"Give, and it will be given to you: good measure, pressed down, shaken together, and running over will be put into your bosom. For with the same measure that you use, it will be measured back to you."*
**Luke 6:38 KJV**

I thank GOD for a changed mindset. By knowing who GOD is; what GOD does; and if it is GOD'S permissible will, I know what HE can do. The same Eld. Frye mentioned earlier in this book, is the same Eld. Frye GOD spoke to and said, **"Poverty is a mindset. Broke is a season. You CHANGE Your Mindset. You CHANGE Your Season."** That applies to challenges given and every situation we have placed ourselves in that can lead to our defeat and possibly our demise. This includes EVERY MANNER of disease and all afflictions. Just like disease and affliction are in small case letters in this book, it is essential that they are placed in small case letters in your mind, action, spirit, and heart. They have no power in an Undefeated Heart that is Protected by the Breastplate of Righteousness. Those wicked words have no strength in a Renewed Mind that is Covered by the Helmet of Salvation. There is no power they can drain if Actions are Activated By Faith. Praise and Worship will defeat those worthless words when Worshiping the FATHER IN Spirit and IN Truth. (**Ephesians 6:11-18, John 4:24**)

I truly believe that the reason why Raiden's two years of Wonderful Life were so Blessed, abundant, and full of life and Faith in GOD is because my Blessed mindset change and because I spoke life and did not treat these two women as if they were about to journey the road of sadness and death.

The journey that I shared with Raiden was purely scriptural. There was no other way to do it, it was our destiny to praise GOD in spite of. In the labor and delivery room, as we prepared to meet Raiden, the room was filled with the melodies of Gospel music. When I gave birth to Raiden, my mother and mother-in-love began to praise GOD and shout—like seriously they took a praise break! This is an awesome memory. Throughout Raiden's life, He was a Praiser. I mean his body would move and bounce while in my arms. There were times when He said Hallelujah; there were times where his hands were busy clapping— on beat!; if I was up praising GOD in our home, at church, at the hospital and Raiden saw, he would lift his arms and cry until I picked him up so we could bounce and praise GOD together. That was my Shouting Partner! I love him so and I thank GOD that I was Blessed to raise him in his two years and two weeks of life in the Fervent Fear of GOD. As mentioned earlier, after Raiden's transition, my Husband Prayed and Gave GOD the GLORY for such an Awesome Wonderful Blessing to Love and Parent Raiden.

Join with me, take this moment to just take a PRAISE BREAK AND GIVE GOD THE GLORY—Turn on some shouting music and Show GOD YOUR Admiration, For GOD IS WORTHY OF ALL THE PRAISE!

*Just in my intermission Praise Break, I just heard Tye Tribbett say, "HE [GOD] does not need our Praise, HE [GOD] deserves it...the rocks will cry out for us if we keep silent!"* [1]

*In my praise, I was able to release to GOD. I implore you before you read any more...if you did not during your Praise, Release to GOD, I encourage you to take this precious time to Release to GOD any setbacks, any doubt, any fear that may be facing you. Turn all of it and Make it Face GOD. List it. Shout it. Write it. Just RELEASE IT and GIVE IT TO GOD.*

*In my praise, my cellular phone began to mess up. For me, this is nothing new. Whenever I seem to get my True praise on while listening to music on a certain website, my phone stops working properly. But devil you cannot take what I need to Release because this belongs to GOD.*

*I now have put a CD in and the first song that plays is "POWER BELONGS TO GOD," by Hezekiah Walker and the Love Fellowship Crusade Choir in their Album, FAMILY AFFAIR.* [2]

*I pray you feel better! Let us continue.*

# 5

## In Time

**Ain't GOD good?!** There are many miracles that I have heard of, but the miracles GOD performed In Raiden's Life makes me want to *Run Til I Finish*! GOD'S Awesome Power gives me an overwhelming smile. Thinking of a smile, GOD blessed Raiden with such an awesome smile. So joyous and determined. GOD chose Raiden to grace this earth to show others that GOD IS REAL and that THE BLOOD OF JESUS STILL WORKS! There is no denying it. The beauty of the whole-almost two years of Raiden being treated for cancer was rarely painted with sorrowful moments. I have more memories of us treating the hospital as if it were our apartment than as if it were a prison.

In August 2016, Raiden was blessed, his stay was short in the Pediatric ICU floor. After four days, he was transported to the Pediatric hematology-oncology floor, where we stayed in the hospital for almost eight weeks. It was a long unexpected amount of time but there is always a blessing in the wilderness. Just like the Israelites, GOD fed us well, we did not thirst for anything, and our feet never swelled! (**Nehemiah 9:21**) We were graced with cable and the internet that also connected to the television, there was a laundry room, I never had to cook a meal, and there was a room phone—and that was just the perks at the hospital. During the second week, my mother-in-love's job blessed my husband and me daily with a meal and even collected money for us! Now that deserves a celebration! Who does that?! GOD was truly in the midst of the whole experience.

Raiden was being Raiden, in great spirits not needing any aid from any medical equipment. When we got to the new floor the doctors ordered oxygen for Raiden. The oxygen ordered was not the type of equipment with two inserts for the nostrils, nor was it the type of equipment that is to be placed over the nose and mouth. The oxygen instead flowed out of a tube that was to be near Raiden. His need for oxygen equipment was not nearly as direr as the day he entered the hospital. GOD did not stop there! GOD Blessed Raiden so much so that within a day or two of transitioning floors, he was breathing on his own without assistance!

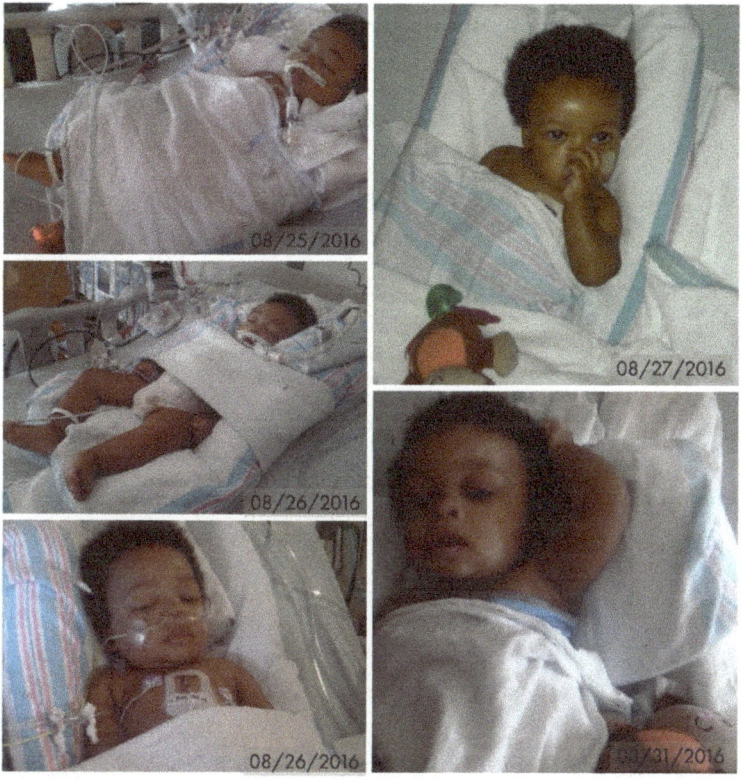

Raiden had surgery the day he was rushed from St. Joseph Mercy hospital into the Mott's Children's Hospital emergency surgery room. This made me nervous and I was not comfortable with this. For Raiden to receive treatment, the doctors informed my husband and me that Raiden would have to get a permanent I.V. placed in his chest. This was one of the hardest things I faced because seeing the Broviac I.V. was a lot to behold. We were responsible to oversee the upkeep of the Broviac when Raiden was at home. Often, when visitors would come,

I would try to make sure that Raiden had on an onesie, not to make others uncomfortable and afraid. It was nothing but GOD'S grace and intervention that Raiden never tugged on the Broviac I.V. tube, I cannot recall any times Raiden even trying to play with the Broviac I.V. The following week, after transitioning floors, Raiden began chemotherapy treatment and responded like a conqueror!

# 6

## More Than Anything

**Yay!** *In Time*, after 7 weeks, **Raiden was released from the hospital!** What a day of Rejoicing! Within the next month, Raiden had doctor appointments and scheduled in-patient stays. Since August 23rd, Raiden had several lumbar punctures in his spine. But I am so grateful, that as far as my husband and I could tell it did not affect Raiden.

For weeks, the doctors began to voice their concern to my husband and me about Raiden's charts, indicating that he had not gone into remission after over a month of chemotherapy. One chart showed that his bone marrow was in remission, but they wanted to see that Raiden's spine and brain had no signs of leukemia. Due to their concern, they decided to increase Raiden's lumbar puncture surgeries twice a week. I was not pleased with this whatsoever, especially since Raiden was days shy of 8 months and I was concerned about any spinal issues it could have caused him later in life. They were persistent but so was I.

The week prior Raiden had a full 24-hour treatment of chemotherapy medicine, this treatment was different from the rest, not just because of the length, but because it caused

Raiden to have mucous membrane build up. Before Raiden could be released from the hospital after that treatment, Raiden had to get another treatment that coincided with the chemotherapy. Afterward, the nurses checked Raiden's blood during certain timed increments until it showed that most of the follow-up treatment cleared his system. When we were released, we were so ecstatic to go home, but when we got home, throughout the night my husband and I heard Raiden wheezing in his sleep and we did not understand why and were quite concerned. While active and awake, there was no recognized sound of wheezing, the wheezing was only heard whenever he lay.

The fourth week in October, on a Monday or Tuesday, Raiden had a scheduled doctor's appointment and a lumbar puncture. My husband and I voiced our concerns about Raiden's wheezing, and I made mention how uncomfortable I felt about Raiden getting this lumbar puncture especially since the anesthesiologist would be giving Raiden anesthesia. The doctors told us Raiden's response to that treatment he received was normal and they insisted that Raiden still get the lumbar puncture. I was not pleased and felt uneasy, however, the procedure still occurred. Before the procedure, Raiden was taken to pre-op, the nurse and anesthesiologist asked if my husband and I had concerns and we relayed to them Raiden's response to the chemotherapy he received days prior.

They continued to prepare Raiden for the lumbar puncture and soon after we left Raiden in the hands of the nurse practitioner and anesthesiologist. As we waited, I told my husband that this procedure was taking longer than normal. In the midst of the longer than normal wait, we go to the cafeteria to get some food, as we are doing so we see one of the nurses that was in the room with Raiden and the nurse tells us that his oxygen level dropped to 40% during the procedure. Thankfully, it went back to normal, but the thoughts were that it occurred due to the mucous membrane build-up from the chemotherapy.

Before we leave, we meet with the doctors once again and they inform us that they wanted to give Raiden another lumbar puncture the next day. I voiced my rejection concerning this. I made it clear to many doctors, that Raiden's life was not in the palm of their hands but GOD'S. I was not a parent operating in fear and quickly obliged with doctors' recommendations. As mentioned, the decisions made concerning Raiden were almost always consulted with the LORD. Within seconds, GOD placed in my spirit to tell them to push that date to Thursday. They agreed.

I love the way GOD works! There had been a lot of attacks coming from the enemy, not just concerning Raiden. I started to get spiritually fed up. That same week, GOD placed it in my spirit to call for a prayer service at the hospital that Friday. This prayer was never centered concerning Raiden. I sent a text to the ones that GOD placed in my spirit to contact.

Thursday, Raiden was still experiencing breathing difficulties and again we voiced it to the doctors; however, they were headstrong on continuing with the procedure. Following, the scheduled doctor's appointment that morning, Raiden was checked in to the hospital as an inpatient, which had been the plan because the following day, the doctor's scheduled to give Raiden more chemotherapy. As we get comfortable in the room, time passes and we are informed that Raiden will not have the treatment in the operating room on the surgery floor as normal, but they would be doing the procedure on the Pediatric hematology-oncology floor, doors away from Raiden's inpatient room.

Before the procedure, the man who was kind to Raiden and our family the day Raiden left St. Joseph Mercy hospital and the same day we arrived at the University of Michigan Mott's Children's hospital stopped by and checked on the three of us and left Raiden with a stuffed bear. After him, a woman came in, who is staff for the hospital's specialized team that has the authorization to give anesthesia and be present during certain procedures. She asked my husband and me to sign this paper, permitting for Raiden to receive anesthesia. Shortly after, Raiden and I were wheeled into the procedure room by my husband. I gave Raiden to the nurses so they could proceed with the procedure and my husband and I stayed in the room. It did not seem to take too long. We soon went back to Raiden's assigned inpatient room.

Not too long after a nurse and aid, prepared Raiden for the following day's chemotherapy by attempting to put a catheter in Raiden. I told them the size that he needed. They did not listen to what I said and tried to insert a catheter too big for Raiden continuously. I repeatedly let them know the size he needed. Several attempts later, they call around to find the accurate size. After inserting the accurate size I made mention to use, the nurse and aide leave the room. My husband and I are now exhausted and allow Raiden to lay in the crib. Before I close my eyes, I send a reminder text about prayer the following day.

As we begin to close our eyes, Raiden begins to cry. Pushing past tiredness, my husband and I, both get up and see Raiden's lips are blue. I freeze, and all rational thoughts seem to escape from me. Thank GOD for my Husband, right away he begins mouth to mouth with Raiden. I run out of the room, I cannot tell you why I initially did run out of the room but as my thoughts come rushing back, I begin to call for help in the hallways. I do not remember returning to the room, but I truly Thank GOD for my husband, he stayed in the room giving Raiden mouth to mouth until the doctors came. I, on the other hand, ran into the arms of one of our favorite nurses and sobbed.

But as I sobbed, GOD reminded me of a testimony that I had just heard of a woman boldly proclaiming about her child who seemed to have been on the brink of death and she spoke to GOD with the boldness of CHRIST. I did just the same. Two months prior, as my pastor and first lady visited Raiden and our family as Raiden was in PICU, GOD revealed to my pastor that GOD was going to make Raiden a star. Having the GOD Given Testimony of the woman and GOD'S Prophetic word spoken by my pastor in the forefront of my mind, I begin to talk to GOD, in the arms of the nurse. I do not recall my exact words, but I do remember, saying to GOD, that it was not time. If GOD took Raiden, then what testimony would spring forth out of Raiden's passing. How could a story end like that make Raiden a star? I regained my strength declaring out loud not caring who heard me, that Raiden was not about to die. After that, I regained my composure.

Then my husband came out, due to the swarm of doctors and nurses that filled one of the two tiniest rooms on the Pediatric hematology-oncology floor. I held my husband in my arms making sure that he was able to have a seat. The hallway was swarmed with nurses and nurse practitioners from the floor with fear in their eyes and tears streaming down their faces. Some asked if I was alright. I told them I was fine with such a smile on my face. I instead was passing out tissues to them. I did not need to fear. Shortly after, amid the mumbling sounds coming from the room, we on the outside, hear a cry come forth out of Raiden and I was even more Joyful. My Husband was a lot more at ease after hearing Raiden's wail.

Raiden was rushed to Pediatric ICU, after being stabilized. They performed tests on Raiden trying to discover why such an occurrence. The following morning during rounds the doctor revealed he had no clue nor any explanation. Which made me glad because I knew this was the doing of my GREAT AND MIGHTY GOD.

My husband and I gathered our belongings and joined Raiden on PICU. The first person I was led to call, if I am not mistaken, was my pastor. I love that though my Pastor and First Lady may have saddened by the news of what had just occurred, they knew not to overwhelm me with it. It probably would have placed me in a stage of panic. Of course, facing such things can bring frantic behavior and worry. But from the beginning, the three of us declared that we were going to believe the report of the LORD and leave it in HIS HANDS.

Was my adrenaline high? Yes. But I was more pumped because I was excited to see yet another Miracle performed by the LORD because I knew that Raiden was coming out of this one.

It was not long after that I called our family. I love them, but I am sure I seemed quite peculiar to them especially when I decided that I was going to go to a revival that night. I needed GOD to move on the behalf of Raiden and I was a firm believer: if you want GOD to move quickly, you have to show HIM that YOU believe that not only that HE can but HE WILL DO IT. I left the room that night, though Raiden was back connected to tubes and wires like in August, He looked peaceful and that was enough confirmation I needed to know that Raiden would be simply fine. Granted he was with his daddy, who was not leaving Raiden's side, and a host of nurses and doctors, but most essential, He was in the HANDS OF A GREAT AND MIGHTY GOD.

What an awesome time I had at church! I received a report from GOD that night that Raiden was healed through Evangelist Thomas. There was no doubt in my mind that her affirmation was completely true and more than likely I gave GOD great praise! With that report in mind, I got back to the hospital and I walked in the ICU room like I was not entering into a hospital room.

The next morning as mentioned, we had discussions with the doctors during morning rounds. In the discussion, we learned that Raiden had a cardiac arrest and respiratory distress and died for a brief period. This shocked me, yet I could not help but be full of joy knowing that GOD'S GREAT AND

MIGHTY POWER BLESSED Raiden to have Victory despite the reports given.

Despite the unexpected occurrence, I never felt led to cancel prayer. However, the prayer which was scheduled to be on the Pediatric hematology-oncology floor was now in an ICU room. Only three people showed up. I remember I did receive a response from one of the others invited and if I am not mistaken someone else may have called to inform me that were not able to attend. I much appreciated that.

First, my mom came, I had started praying and she joined in. As I continued in prayer, I remember quoting a part of scripture from King Jehoshaphat when he confronted the LORD concerning Judah. *"O LORD God of our fathers, art not thou God in heaven?"* (2 Chronicles 20:6 KJV). Then King Jehoshaphat listed the GREAT AND MIGHTY WORKS GOD had performed previously. Praise be to GOD, perhaps days or a week or so prior I had just learned that story in the bible as I listened to Pastor John K. Jenkins preach.

My childhood friend—that GOD allowed me to connect back with as we both served as school bus drivers at the same location—sent me videos of Pastor Jenkins to encourage me either late August or early September and I am so glad she did! As I continued to pray my Pastor and First Lady joined in. My pastor anointed the bed Raiden was sleeping in, the rails, and he anointed Raiden. The prayer was so AWESOME! Imagine, GOD had me call a prayer meeting. My thoughts were that it was for us to pray for the saints due to the messiness of the enemy. However, all along it was for Raiden.

# 7

## Where Would I Be

**GOD used my Pastor again to confirm that Raiden's life will be well-known, and he told me that I must write a book.** Also, my pastor added that *More Than Anything* he felt no death or dismay, just peace. Which illustrated the same way GOD was allowing me to feel.

Hours later, Raiden's main hematology-oncology doctor entered the room. She wanted to talk to my husband and I; she informed us that the results from the lumbar puncture came back and showed no signs of leukemia in Raiden's spine and brain. Raiden was in remission!!!

Two months Prior on August 26, Raiden was diagnosed with leukemia. On the 27th of August, after four days of being on the ICU floor, Raiden was transported to the Pediatric hematology-oncology floor. Two months later, on October 27th, Raiden was sent, once again, to the PICU. The following day, on October 28th, 2016 Raiden was in remission! 26. 27. 28. It was like GOD brought us back, to the place where a terminal report was given to rewind time and erase what was first mentioned to replace it with HIS GOOD NEWS!

Ain't GOD GOOD!

*Psalm 91:3-16* ³*Surely THE FATHER shall deliver Raiden from the snare of the fowler, and from the noisome pestilence.* ⁴*THE FATHER shall cover thee with HIS Feathers, and under HIS Wings shalt Raiden trust: THE FATHER'S Truth shall be Raiden's shield and buckler.* ⁵*Raiden shalt not be afraid for the terror by night; nor for the arrow that flieth by day;* ⁶*Nor for the pestilence that walketh in darkness; nor for the destruction that wasteth at noonday.* ⁷*A thousand shall fall at Raiden's side, and ten thousand at Raiden's right hand; but it shall not come nigh Raiden.* ⁸*Only with Raiden's eyes shalt he behold and see the reward of the wicked.* ⁹*Because Raiden hast made THE LORD, which is Raiden's father and mother refuge, even the most High, his habitation;* ¹⁰*There shall no evil befall Raiden, neither shall any plague come nigh Raiden's dwelling.* ¹¹*For THE FATHER shall give HIS angels charge over Raiden, to keep him in all thy ways.* ¹²*They shall bear Raiden up in their hands, lest he dash his foot against a stone.* ¹³*Raiden shalt tread upon the lion and adder: the young lion and the dragon shalt Raiden trample under feet.* ¹⁴*Because Raiden hath set his love upon THE FATHER, therefore will THE FATHER deliver Raiden: THE FATHER will set him on high, because Raiden hath known THE FATHERS NAME.* ¹⁵*Raiden shall call upon THE FATHER, and HE will answer him: THE FATHER will be with Raiden in Trouble; THE FATHER will Deliver Raiden, and Honour Raiden.* ¹⁶*With long life will THE FATHER satisfy Raiden, and shew Raiden THE FATHER'S salvation.*

# 8

## Put Your Hands Together

"**Is this him?**" the Head Pediatric hematology-oncology doctor at another children's hospital asked me. Before meeting Raiden, the doctor read over Raiden's medical paperwork. After walking into the room, the head doctor admitted to being shocked and amazed at how Raiden looked and behaved especially after experiencing a cardiac arrest.

# EVIDENCE TARTT

# 9

## Right Now

*2019*

***A day in April/May:***

*I do not know when the last page was written but it has been thirteen days short of 5 months since I looked at VICTORY IS MINE. I believe, it has been a year this month since this book received its first word.*

*To be honest I have been dreading May. Last year's Mother's Day took a toll on me. I am grateful that I did not break.*

***A day in May:***

*Hello, again. I am now ending the month of May by the grace of GOD. This book is a book that only GOD is going to give me the strength to write. But guess what Mother's Day this year was an AWESOME Day!*

**Last year started great also...**

## *2018*

*I do not remember most details concerning 2018's Mother's Day. I went to my church, Greater St. Joseph Tabernacle, and I am sure I had an Awesome time in the LORD! After service, I went to a restaurant in Southfield, MI to pick up Mother's Day Carryout dinner to enjoy with my Mom and younger siblings. The drive to my mom was normal, I would not be surprised if I was debating to myself how long I would spend at my mom's because my ultimate plan was to spend time at Raiden's gravesite. GOD, A blanket, myself, and the ground. This was what I was looking forward to. I had hoped to leave my mom's house while the daylight still shined because I had even planned to stay at Raiden's gravesite for a couple of hours if not more. I was having such a fun time with my family, I left extremely late that the sky was starting to darken. I cannot recall for sure, but rain may have begun to fall and sprinkle. My mom's house is about a 7-minute drive from Raiden's gravesite. Within those seven minutes, the sky completely darkened. However, this did not stop me. I was determined, I was going to spend time close to my son. Nothing was going to interrupt my plans.*

*Unfortunately, I should have chosen another day. This was my first time visiting the site since his Homegoing Service. As I pulled into the gravesite, the daylight had completely been pulled away.*

*Though it was pitch dark, I was yet determined. I believe I positioned the car to face the gravesite with my car's bright lights on, which looked creepy, I am sure. My husband and I purposely chose to have Raiden's plot right next to a tree. The tree is huge! And at night, it is not as pleasant looking as it is in the sunshine.*

*I leave the car and I am near, if not under the tree and I do not know where Raiden is. There was no label stating where he was. I do not know the worst thing for a mother to face on Mother's Day, but if there is a list this should be added. In the dark, looking for my son, not able to hold him because instead the ground is holding him.*

*Raiden, who I have not seen in months. And now I have lost him. Twice. From wandering around a tree to driving home, I do not have much recollection other than screaming and hyperventilating. I can remember nearing the exit that merges to the street that leads to our home and not recalling the drive.*

*I was hoarse with a great headache. Not an intelligent move. Would I do it again? No, because after that night I almost went mad in May.*

## *2019*

*Last year's Mother's Day may be hard for those who interact with me to believe because too many assume I am resilient. Not saying that I am not, but in actuality, I am not. Only through CHRIST can I ever fit this description. GOD Allows JESUS' Strength to Hold me and HIS Peace to Live in me and HE gifted me with HIS HOLY SPIRIT to rest in me to bring me comfort when I receive it. There have been times when I did not want to receive it because I wanted to be depressed. Can you imagine? I wanted to be depressed. I wanted to hurt. I believe it was the last Sunday in April when I can last recall me willing to push away GOD to accept depression.*

*I was subconsciously and at times consciously getting my mind ready for another May. My dad was not doing well. I was experiencing car issues that kept me tardy to church.*

*On this particular Sunday, with yet another car dilemma, my mom took pity and allowed me to use her car. The drive to church was going well, I was late, but I was confident that I would enjoy a portion of the service. As I drove the highway, The HOLY SPIRIT gave me warning to stay on the highway I was traveling. I disregarded his heeding and took another way. As I detoured, merging onto another highway, I soon got caught in backed-up-construction-traffic. I am late but I try not to get too discouraged. Soon after, we were barely moving. When we did start to move, majority of the exits were blocked, including my exit that led to church. 'Okay that is fine,' so I think, 'I will get off at the next one.' Closed. The next one after was open but it took about 7 minutes or more to get off the small exit ramp. After exiting the ramp, I was still losing the advantage of time, if I recall correctly, it took even longer to make a left turn. By this time, many streams of tears were coming down my face, each tear led to a flood of remorse, which I was drowning in. Throughout all this, I was still hoping to just merge back on the highway travelling the opposite way.*

*Nope. I was so overwhelmed that returning highway was becoming way too complicated. I was beyond frustration and my memory of how to get back to the highway was failing me. By this point, I was probably yelling. Thinking about May. Thinking about my Husband and our Marriage. Thinking about Raiden. Thinking about my financial status. Thinking about how I was residing with my parents, not having my own place to live. Thinking about my disobedience to GOD. GOD spoke to me and said Worship me. I refused. Ten to twenty minutes prior or maybe right after I dropped off my mom at her church, I was led to listen to her new CD instead of the radio. I was jamming on my way to church at first. By this time, after all the turmoil, my favorite song played. For a while, this was my Hype Song. Not that day. I was sort of trying to get in the mood of the song, but I decided to feel defeated instead of Victorious as the song encouraged. I think I was just ready to get depressed. I was dreading May, ready for the worse.*

### *2019*

*Today is May 27th, and I can Victoriously say that I am in my right mind! I cannot recall any days this month like the Sunday in April. My Mother's Day was good! I did not visit Raiden's grave site on Mother's Day, but I think I went the day or some days after and it ended well. GOD placed me on a fast and I sought HIM prior to the days leading up to Mother's Day. Grateful that I did.*

### *2020*

*Two days have transferred to the past. Today is Tuesday, May 12, 2020. On May 10, 2020, I Celebrated another Mother's Day. Symptoms of depression tried to creep in last month. But Praise Be To GOD, I can still yet Put My Hands Together and Give MY FATHER, Praise.*

# 10

## Run To You

**Be not deceived, for THE LORD OUR GOD never operates in the realm of coincidences but much care springs forth from HIS hidden mysterious plan.** *Right Now*, I have not arrived at the full explanation of why my husband and I were chosen by GOD to birth and raise someone as Miraculous and Rambunctious as our Beautiful Son, Raiden. Although there are still pieces to the puzzle that are awaiting their turn to be placed in the right slot, I am honored to know that GOD saw my husband's seed as blessed and my womb as worthy to carry a Blessing from conception to labor. I am honored that GOD also knew that HE fully equipped us to love Raiden from conception to GLORY.

Can I be honest? This month marks two years of the first word typed for Victory Is Mine and I am just beginning page 21. This book is difficult to complete but it is not Impossible. I know that JESUS' strength, the prayers of the Righteous, and Speaking out Raiden's testimony will help me to overcome.

On March 11, 2018, I was to portray a woman from history that I had grown to admire within the last few years of that date. Weeks before my reenactment of this woman's life, there was an envelope being passed around to the women of our church. We were expected to pull out one of the many small sheets of paper in the envelope, open the folded sheet of paper, read the name of the person written on the sheet of paper, and study and prepare to act out the biblical woman listed.

The envelope came to me, I grabbed a sheet of paper within the envelope, unfolded the sheet of paper, then I read the name written on the paper: **Hannah**. I was so excited! I knew she was once barren and was blessed by GOD to conceive not just one child but seven. The first was Samuel who she made a vow to GOD to give Samuel back to GOD and Hannah kept her vow to GOD. Some researchers say by the age of two or three, Hannah relinquished her "rights" as Samuel's caregiver and gave Samuel fully back to GOD to live out the ministry GOD had planned for him.

The night before, March 11th, I went to bed later than planned. My mother and I were listening to worship music that was created to heal the soul. The next morning, I prepared Raiden and I for service. I had been uneasy for the last few days, the air of death weighed heavy.

I went to church that day expecting a miracle. I was depending greatly on this scripture:

*"Is any sick among you? let him call for the elders of the church; and let them pray over him, anointing him with oil in the name of the Lord"*
**James 5:14**

I was being tormented with fear. Screaming to GOD for a word as I drove the highway leading to the church. Service, I believe, was good. As we drew near to the end of service, my pastor was led in THE SPIRIT to pray for Raiden, who is his Godson. He called his wife, Raiden's Godmother, me, Raiden's other Godfather, and four elders of the church that held an immense amount of love for Raiden in their hearts.

I held Raiden, then I was to pass Raiden to one of the ministers. That minister passed Raiden to the next minister. The next minister passed Raiden to the minister beside him. He then passed Raiden. The eight of us, including my pastor, held and prayed for Raiden twice in the full circle of 8. I perceived a New Beginning. My confidence returned to Raiden's Healing.

The service eventually ended, and now we waited and prepared for the second service conducted by the Women's department. Women were dressing in fabrics to enhance the visual of their performance. I cannot remember if I wore any theatrical wear, but I believe I did a decent job playing the role of Hannah. I acted out 1 Samuel 1:10-11, where Hannah was praying to GOD THE FATHER to bless her womb with a child and in that same prayer, she vowed to give the child, she petitioned for, back to GOD all the days of his life.

*"And she was in bitterness of soul, and prayed unto the Lord, and wept sore.*
*And she vowed a vow, and said, O Lord of hosts, if thou wilt indeed look on the affliction of thine handmaid, and remember me, and not forget thine handmaid, but wilt give unto thine handmaid a man child, then I will give him unto the Lord all the days of his life, and there shall no razor come upon his head."*
**1 Samuel 1:10-11 KJV**

# 11

## Celebrate—Reprise

**After, I ended my portrayal.** I left the church with Raiden heading to the hospital. Raiden's doctor requested that I bring Raiden into the hospital after they received his lab results from the previous day. His counts were extremely high. Raiden's white blood cells were rising to the amounts in the days of August 2016. I was assured that bringing him the next day on Sunday would be fine. I was instructed to bring Raiden through the ER because he did not have a scheduled in-patient appointment. For hours we were in one of the University of Michigan Mott's Children hospital's emergency department rooms.

While there, I made mention to the doctors of some concerns I had concerning Raiden's breathing for the last couple of weeks. These same concerns I made mention to Raiden's doctors weeks prior. When Raiden exhaled, his stomach protruded out greatly. This concerned me greatly. The emergency doctors quickly performed an x-ray. The results were alarming. Raiden had pneumonia and one of his lungs was greatly affected by it.

I believe it was in the wee hours of the next morning or at least close to midnight when we were brought to the Pediatric hematology-oncology floor—where Raiden normally goes if being hospitalized. His hospital visits were becoming weekly stays after or little before his 2nd birthday on February 28th, 2018. The night of March 11th, or the early, early hours of March 12th, Raiden was his feisty 2-year-old self; however, he lacked an appetite. I tried to feed him, but He refused, "No!" Pushing away my efforts to feed him. Although Raiden had a lot of spunk, he was not going to let himself be separated from me. He rested on me as I rested in the reclining chair. At the hospital two things became ritual for Raiden and I, well actually 3. One, Raiden loved the Berenstain Bears, so we watched that more than perhaps any other child catered show. He loved the Berenstain Bears so much that we would play the theme song to keep Raiden calm when his blood was being drawn. The second was faithfully watching Pastor John K. Jenkins from First Baptist Church of Glenarden. Raiden could be sleeping and if he heard Pastor John K. Jenkins' voice, he was bound to want to wake and watch. But at night, we would close our eyes and allow the melodic voices of The Brooklyn Tabernacle Choir rock our weary bodies to sleep. That night, we slept pretty well.

I cannot recall why I woke up, but I noticed that it seemed like the fluid levels that the doctor ordered were not adequately being pushed through Raiden's I.V. I became a little concerned. The nurse was coming in and out the room checking the fluids levels if I recall, I voiced my concern and she then adjusted them. Moments later the most terrifying moment in my life occurred.

Raiden began beating on my chest screaming my name, "Mama. Mama. Mama." I called the nurse and I do not recall much after that because Raiden calmed down. Sometime between that moment and the morning, Raiden was transported from my arms to the hospital room's crib. Raiden threw up and had diarrhea. I believe Raiden had a couple more bouts and we kept changing his sheets. But Raiden slept through all of this. The nurses again kept popping in and out of the room not saying much to me. I prayed. I meditated. I danced. I listened to the word of GOD. I sang songs. Raiden was calm. The chaplain came to visit and check on me. I was calm. We talked. As he left, He kept speaking 'Shalom' over Raiden.

I do not know how many hours later, but as my pastor and my first lady (His wife), and I communed face to face—they came to the hospital after I had called them to pray for Raiden. My pastor could sense my spirit was perplexed so he asked if I would like them to come to the hospital and I said yes—perhaps after an hour of their visit the nurses and doctors ran into the room. The doctors from PICU to be exact. I knew they were ICU doctors because they had worked with Raiden many times before. I saw them and began wondering what is going on and what has happened.

My phone began to ring, and my husband said that someone from the hospital phoned him and said that Raiden was dying, and he needed to hurry and get to the hospital. By then I was exceedingly perplexed. I did what I knew best, I prayed. I prayed aloud to GOD, as it felt like an innumerable amount of trained hospital officials galloped in and out of the hospital room. I tried my best to not allow the cold chills to overwhelm me. To the best I knew how I remained copasetic, excited because I knew GOD was about to perform a Victory for Raiden yet again. I believe I even started singing the song, "Victory Is Mine" because I felt Victory chills moving across my body.

"Mama. Mama. Mama." Were the last words I heard our beautiful baby boy boast.

That morning before all this occurred, I called a meeting with the doctors. For Raiden to start chemotherapy again. After the doctors left the room. I began to speak with GOD. I asked if I heard him wrong and if HE did say end chemotherapy and start alternative treatment. I needed a sign. I can honestly say that if there was any way I could change the outcome, now, I would. For many months, Raiden's last moments replayed in my head. It took longer to sleep. More time was given to concentrate on how I needed to maneuver the highways and byways.

However, Victory did come for Raiden:

***"O, death where is thy sting? O, grave where is thy victory? But thanks be to God, which giveth Raiden the Victory through our Lord Jesus Christ."***
**1 Corinthians 15:55, 57 KJV**

To this day, many including myself, play the what-ifs concerning Raiden in our thoughts. But just like me, many also Celebrate GOD for Raiden's life. I have heard many miraculous testimonies and Raiden's life is one that many hold on to this very day. From birth to two years and two weeks, Raiden had a major impact on every life he encountered.

I Celebrate GOD because HE saw that it was perfect to grant my husband and I permission to love and raise Raiden.

# REFERENCES

Introduction: 1 Cory Asbury. (2017). Reckless Love. Bethel Music Publishing, Watershed Music Group, Richmond Park Publishing

Um Good: 1 Bergren, L. T., & Bryant, L. J. (2000). *God Gave Us You* (1st ed.). WaterBrook Press.

Um Good: 2 Owens, C. C. (2011). *The 40-Day Surrender Fast*. Van Haren Publishing.

Um Good: 3 Kesha Trippett. Daughters of The King Daily Devotionals.

Um Good: 4 Smokie Norful. (2006). Life Changing. EMI Gospel Records.

Run Til I Finish: 1 Tye Tribbett. (2014). Robert Maxwell [YouTube Channel]. Retrieved from https://youtu.be/4Vq__t9iZqQ

REFERENCES

Run Til I Finish: 2 Hezekiah Walker & The Love Fellowship Crusade Choir. (1999). Family Affair. Zomba Recording Corporation.

Meet Evidence: 1 Priscilla Shirer. (n.d). Going Beyond Ministries with Prisicilla Shirer [YouTube Channel]. Retrieved from https://youtu.be/Ewi2iTi3Ec8

www.chapter13publishing.com

Books available to read by Evidence Tartt:

Victory Is Mine
Victory Is Yours
Victory Is Ours

Do It For The Vine: I AM Gonna Do It
Do It For The Vine: I AM Now

Hear—JESUS
Heed—JESUS
Have GOD'S WAY—JESUS
Heal—JESUS

## Meet Evidence

In the fall of 2016, GOD called Evidence Tartt to write a book recognizing the GLORY of HIM working through the Miraculous life of her son. Prior to THE FATHER changing her name, Evidence went by the name Ebony. In the season, THE FATHER revealed to her that she would author a book concerning her son, Ebony was excited and thought that this book would unfold the harsh treatment she felt her son was receiving under the care of medical staff. She was continuously jotting mental notes of every mistake made.

In the season of cold bitterness, she failed to realize that the book was not a gossip column but a Gospel Corroboration. Her husband and herself had been chosen to be the parents of a child that GOD THE FATHER found precious and worthy to reveal his love and protection through even when some may not normally expect to see HIS Goodness when a child is deemed terminally ill.

In the late spring of 2018, Evidence was spending time with THE FATHER and discovered in passage—while listening to Priscilla Shirer[1]— the words, "Hear ye HIM." Evidence decided to take those three seeded words and plant them and 2 years later, those words sprouted into a Four Book Devotional, a Three Book Series Dedicated to THE FATHER reflecting the Amazing Life of her and her husband's son and how He was used by GOD to prune twigs to make room for Graceful Fruit to grow, and a great collection of many more GOD Revealing Reads.

Evidence Tartt is a woman, of faith, honored to be called GOD's daughter. A wife, of Abounding Love, that has learned how to make her husband top priority, under the leadership of The Holy Ghost and with GOD's Graceful Love—because there is no greater love than that. She is the proud mother, of Growing Wisdom and Never-failing Love, to their son, Raiden; and a mother not ashamed to admit the sinful flaws that she committed to when, in 2012, unfortunately declining the first time GOD welcomed her to motherhood.

Evidence has been blessed to be called JESUS' little sister and she prays that everyone that reads the books GOD has called her to write and those who may not read can be called her sibling through the fellowship of JESUS CHRIST.

Lightning Source UK Ltd.
Milton Keynes UK
UKHW020437210820
368556UK00009B/617